for Jenn

Copyright © Jeremy Holmes 2016

Outside The Lines Press

www.outsidethelinespress.com

ALL RIGHTS RESERVED

This book contains material protected under International and Federal Copyright Laws and Treaties. Any unauthorized reprint or use of this material is prohibited. No part of this book may be reproduced or transmitted in any form or by any means, electronic or mechanical, including photocopying, recording, or by any information storage and retrieval system without express written permission from the author / publisher.

Written and Illustrated by Jeremy Holmes

ISBN: 978-0-9949240-6-3

Pun, Pun Rudolph

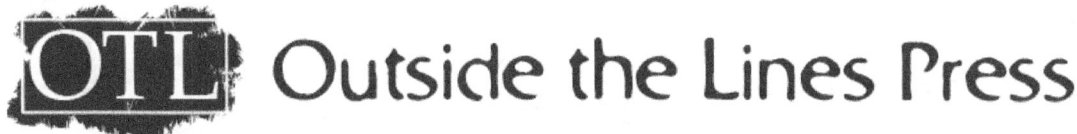
Outside the Lines Press

kung fu-dolph

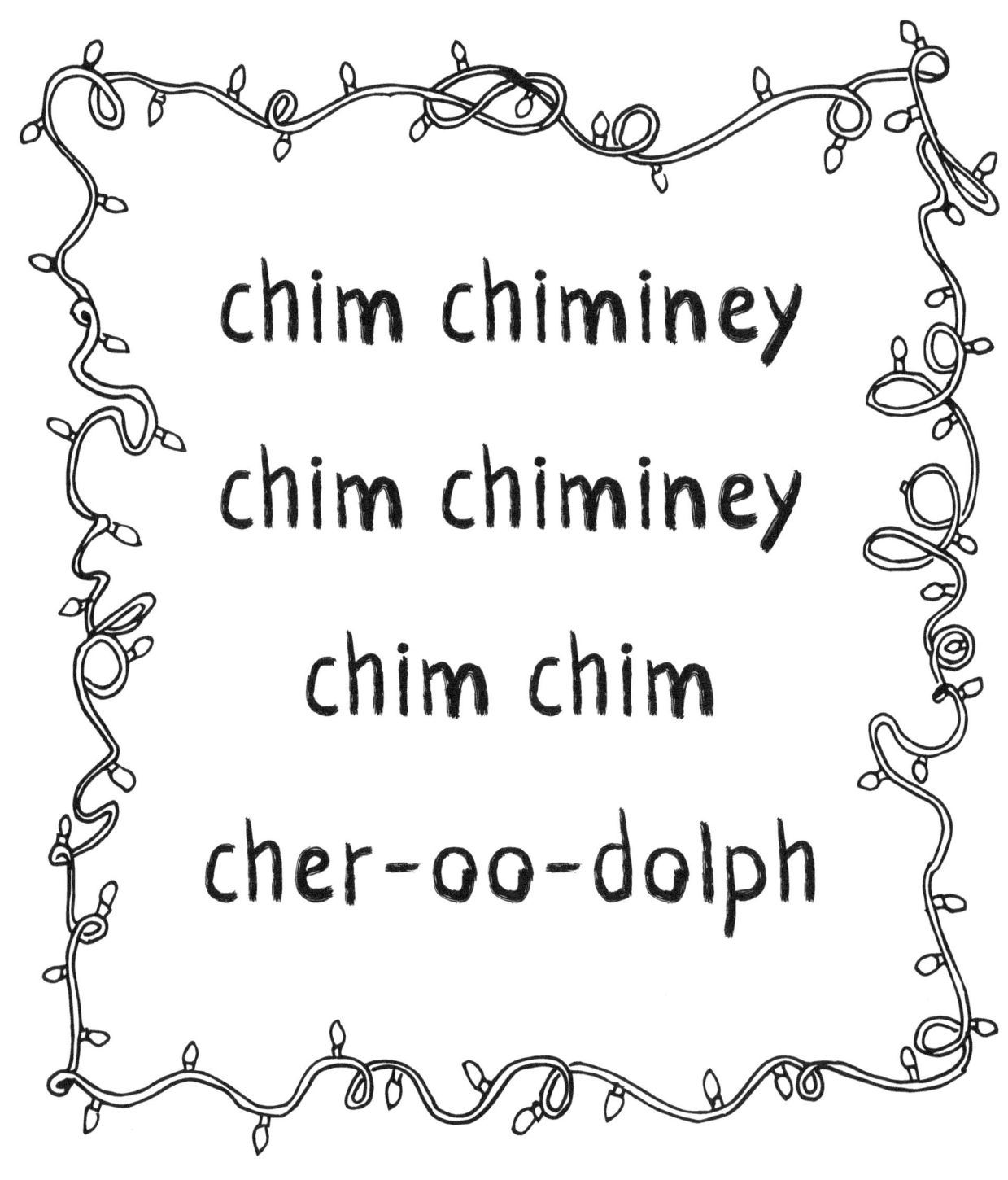

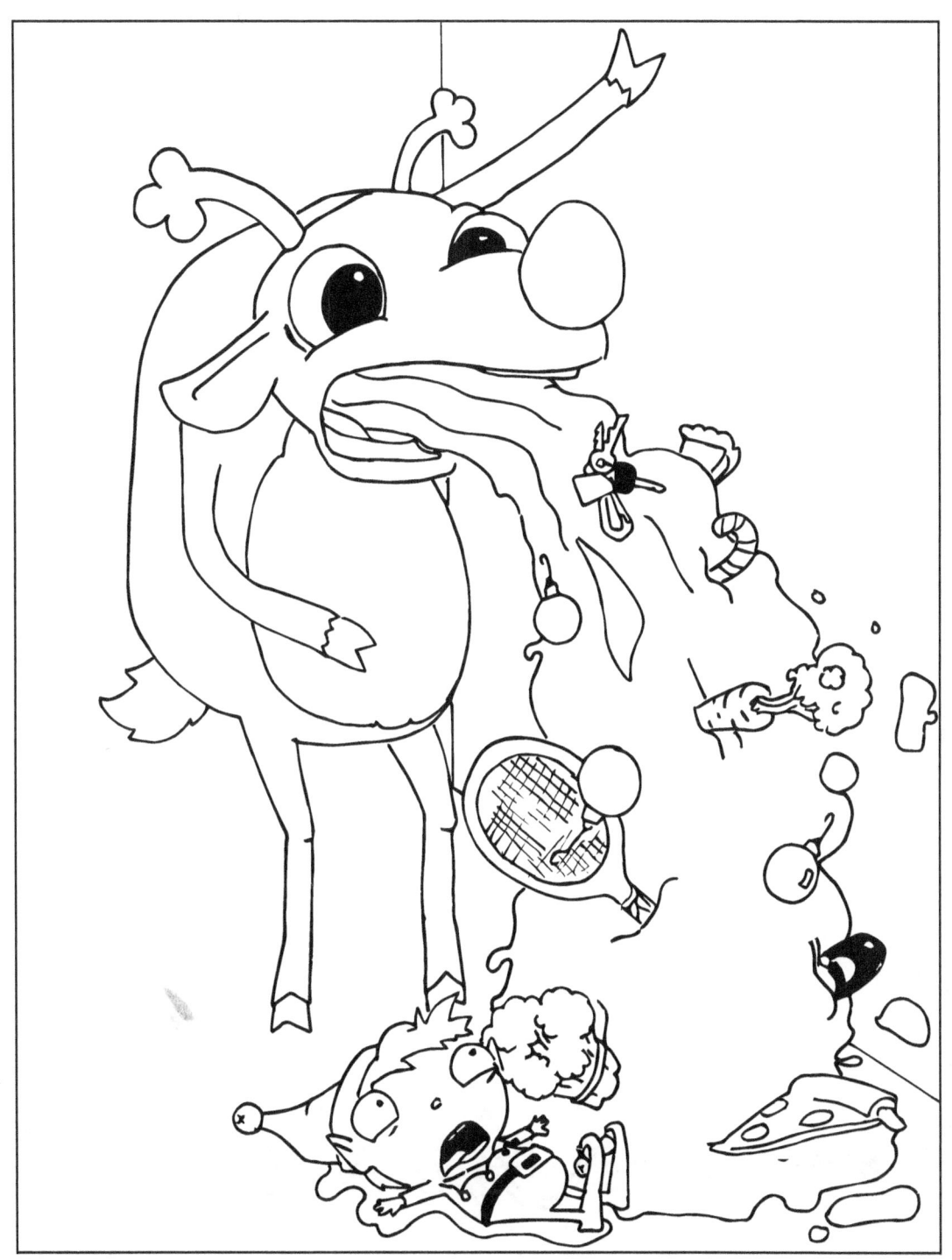

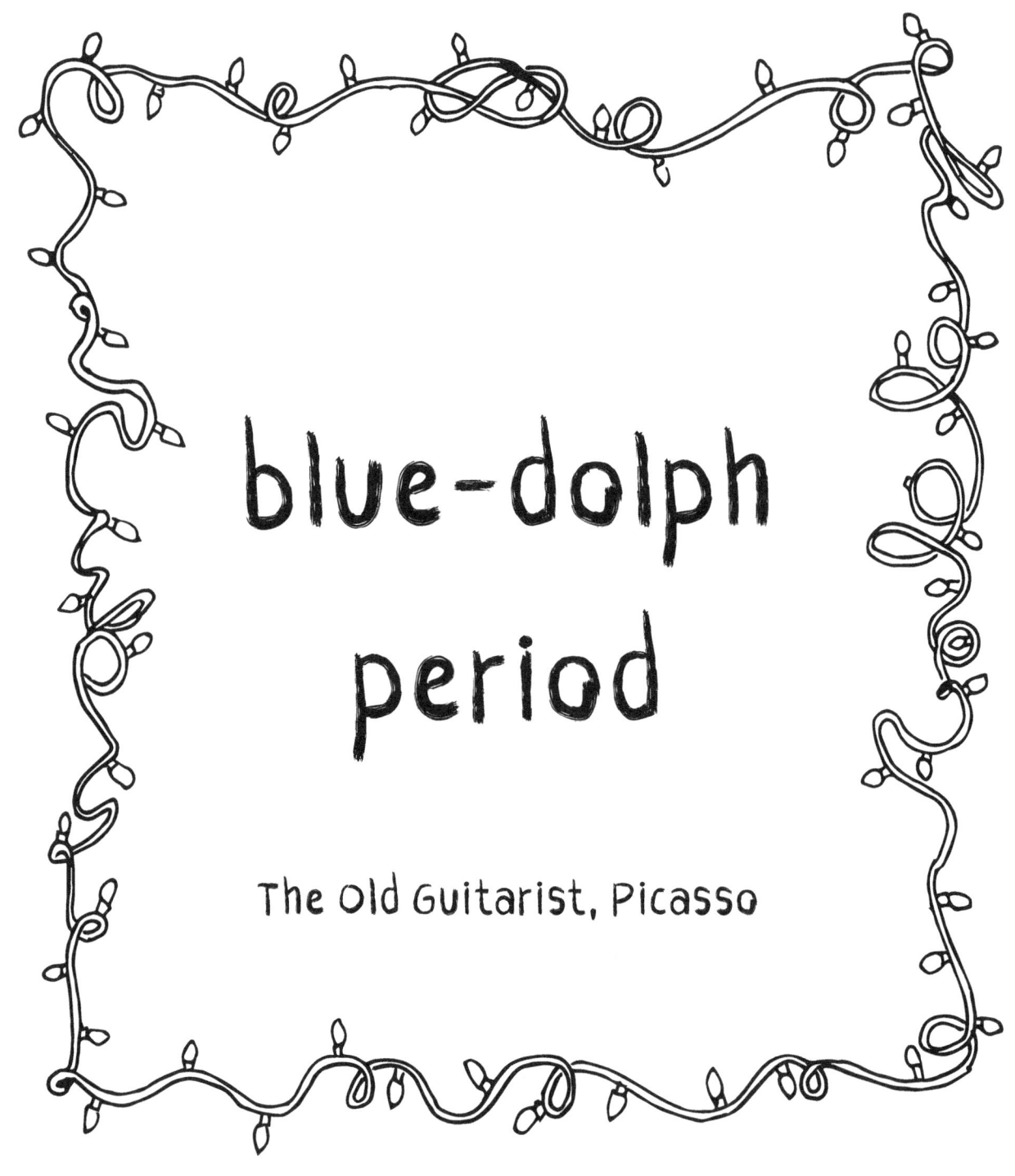

blue-dolph period

The Old Guitarist, Picasso

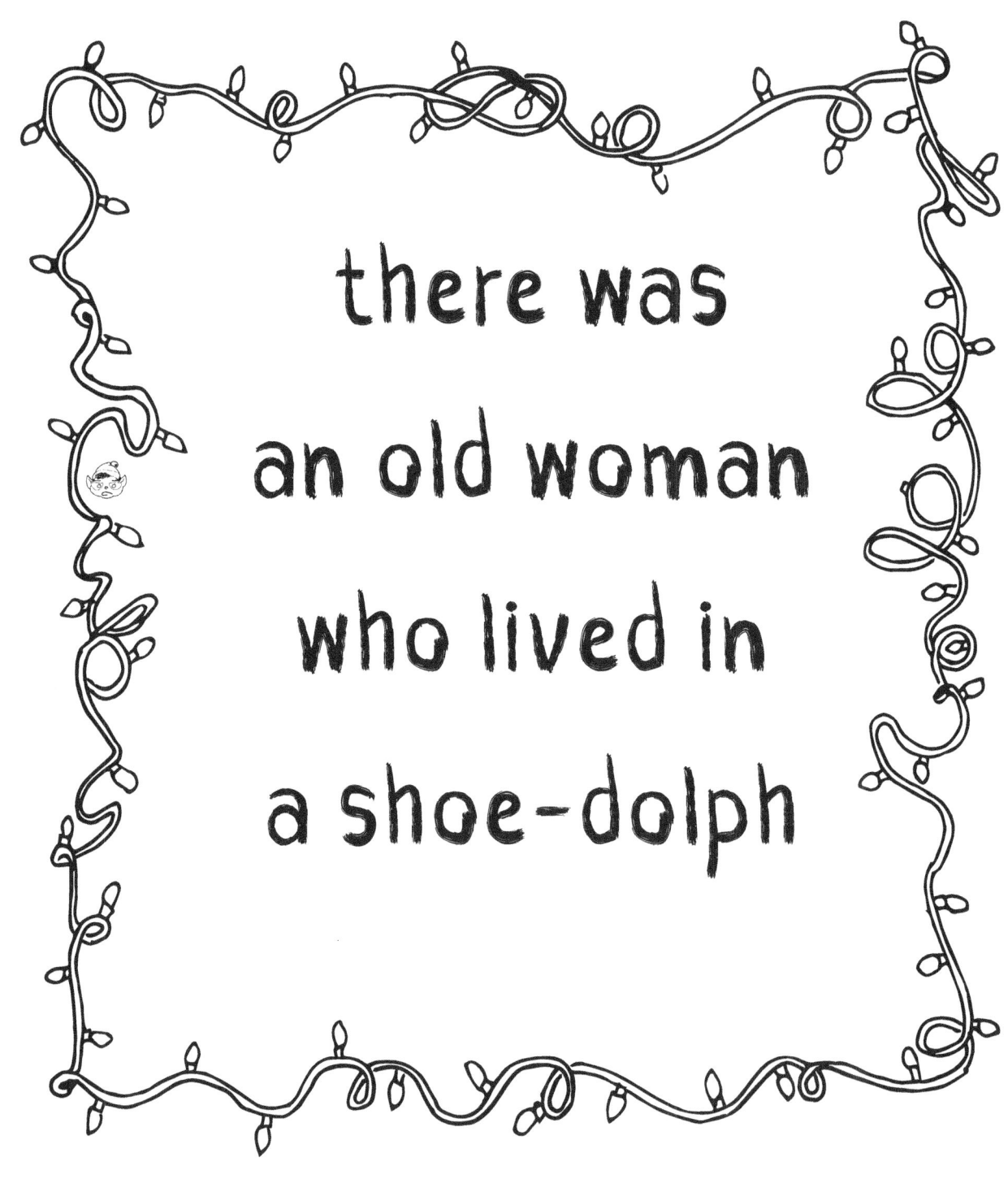

there was

an old woman

who lived in

a shoe-dolph

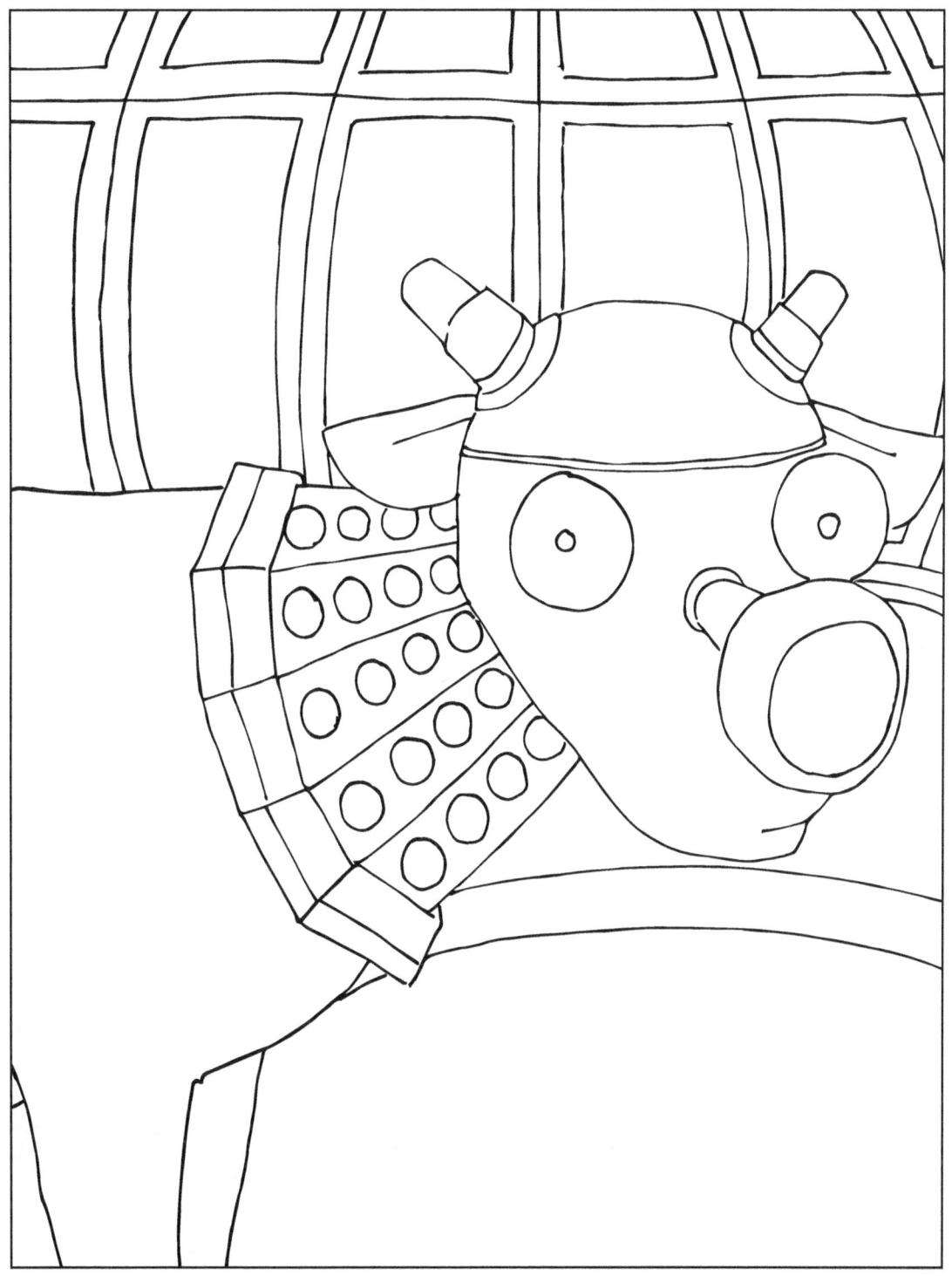

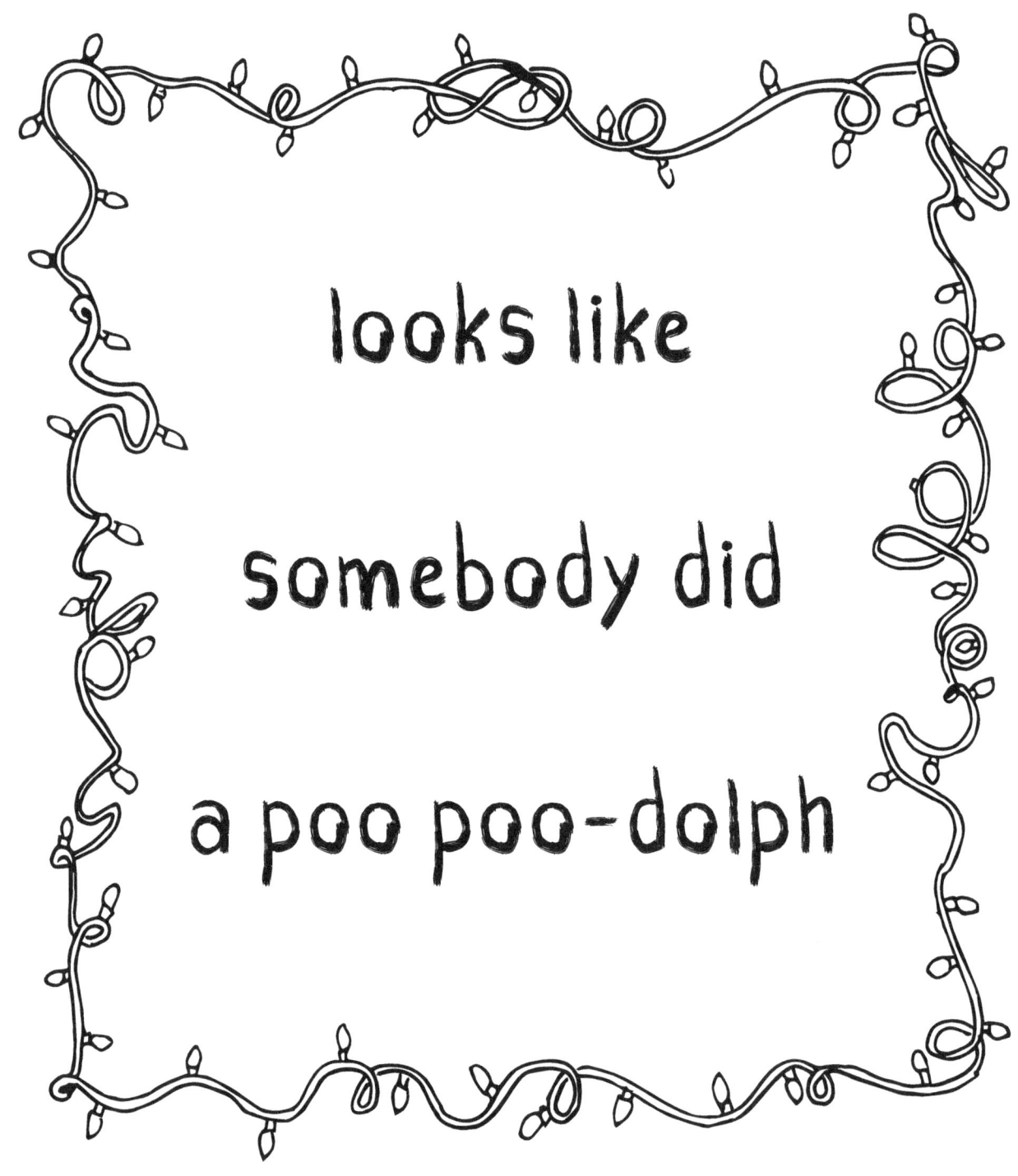

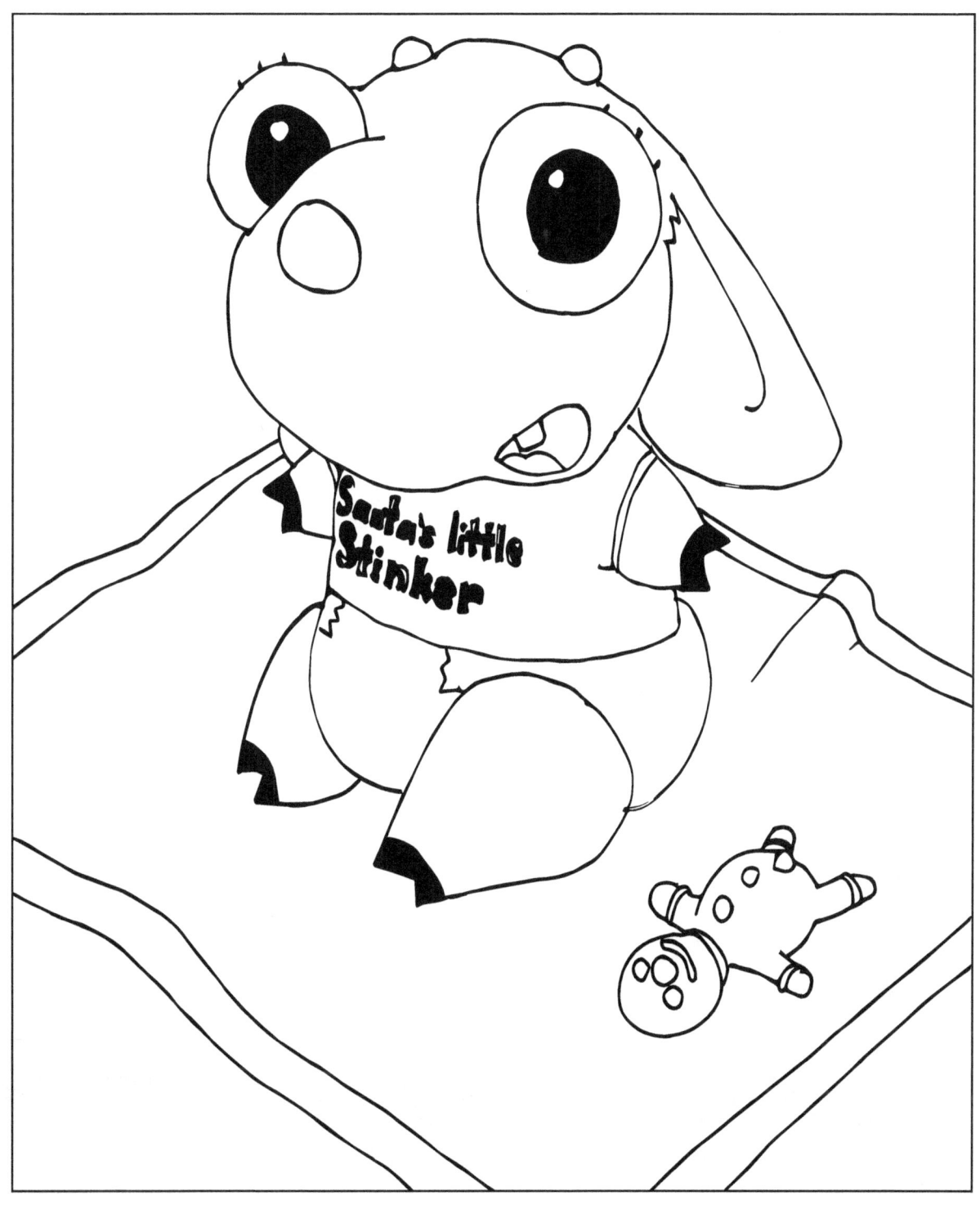

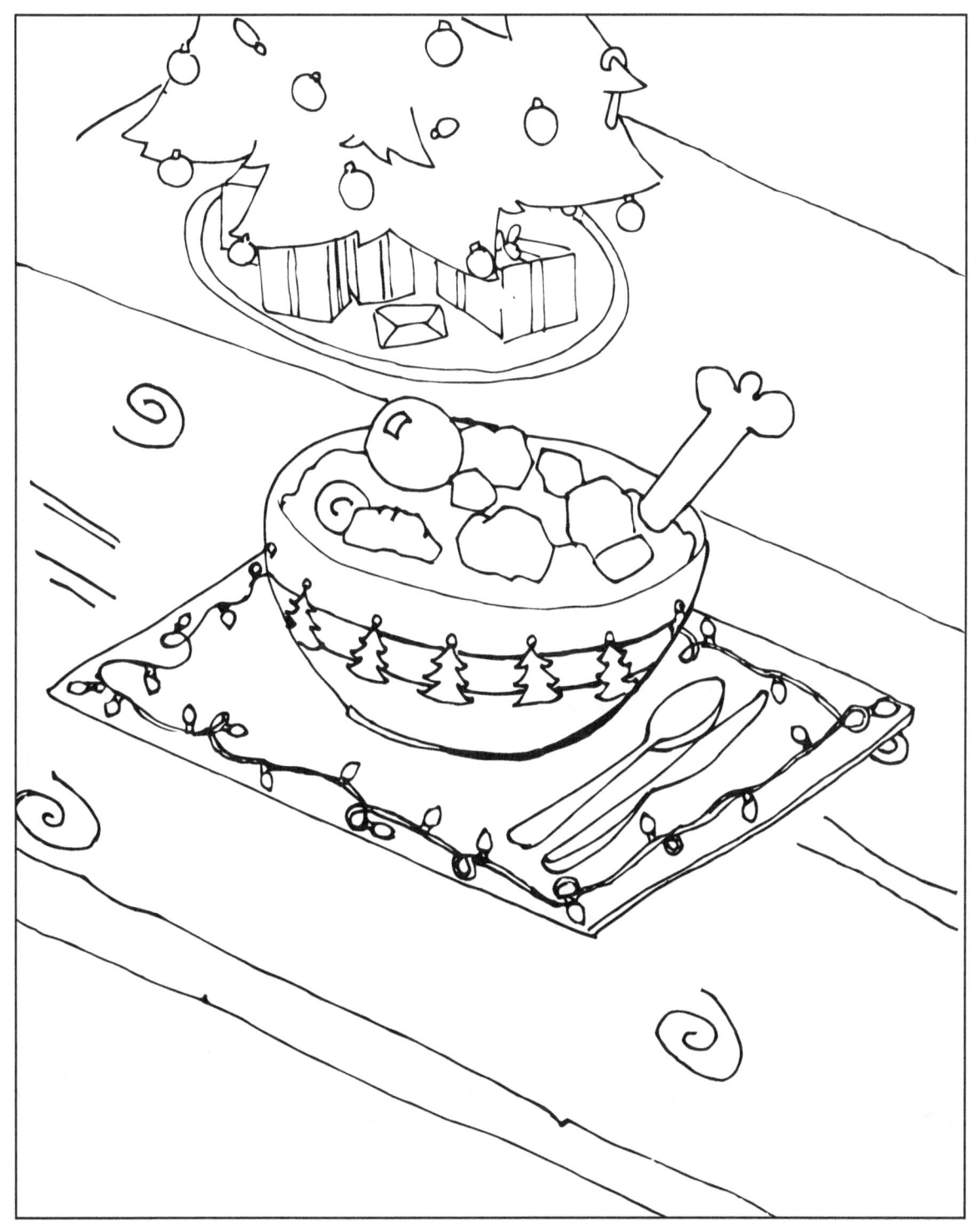

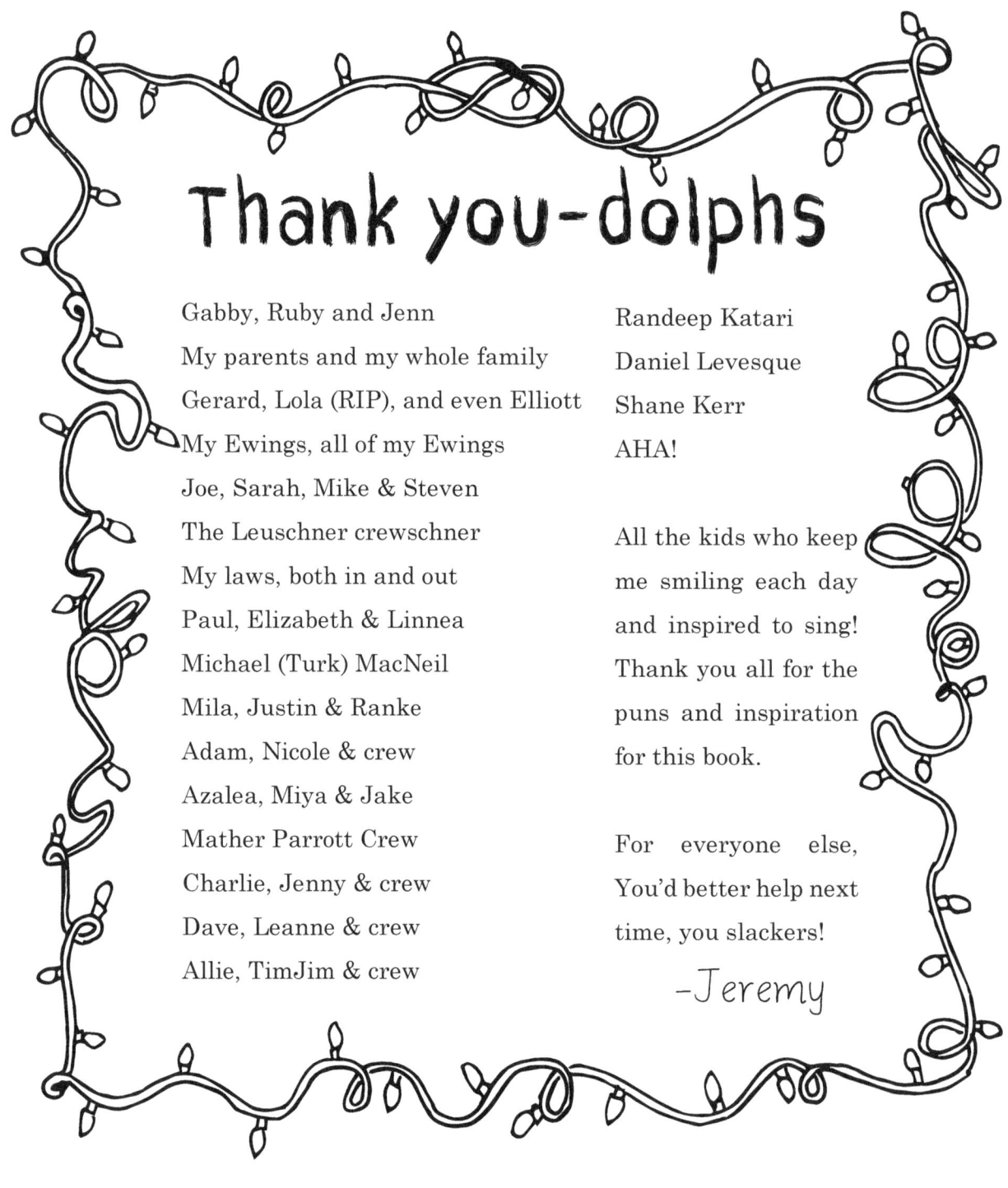

More coloring books from Outside the Lines Press:

Outside the Lines Press

Did you enjoy the family friendly humor of Jeremy Holmes? If so, check out his children's album titled "The Little Ditties." It won an East Coast Music Award (Children's Recording of the Year). It's made for kids, parents, grandparents and anyone in between who loves to dance, sing, stomp, clap or sing their way through the day. Available on iTunes and Bandcamp.

the end

www.ingramcontent.com/pod-product-compliance
Lightning Source LLC
Chambersburg PA
CBHW080413300426
44113CB00015B/2506